MAGIC GEMS

JOURNEY THROUGH THE WATERFALL

Payal Doshi

AF661304

MAGIC GEMS

JOURNEY THROUGH THE WATERFALL

PAYAL DOSHI

SCHOLASTIC INC

If you purchased this book without a cover, you should be aware that this book is stolen property. It was reported as "unsold and destroyed" to the publisher, and neither the author nor the publisher has received any payment for this "stripped book."

Copyright © 2026 by Payal Doshi

Illustrations by Heather Burns, copyright © 2026 by Scholastic Inc.

All rights reserved. Published by Scholastic Inc., *Publishers since 1920.* SCHOLASTIC and associated logos are trademarks and/or registered trademarks of Scholastic Inc.

The publisher does not have any control over and does not assume any responsibility for author or third-party websites or their content.

No part of this publication may be reproduced, stored in a retrieval system, or transmitted in any form or by any means, electronic, mechanical, photocopying, recording, or otherwise, or used to train any artificial intelligence technologies, without written permission of the publisher. For information regarding permission, write to Scholastic Inc., Attention: Permissions Department, 557 Broadway, New York, NY 10012.

This book is a work of fiction. Names, characters, places, and incidents are either the product of the author's imagination or are used fictitiously, and any resemblance to actual persons, living or dead, business establishments, events, or locales is entirely coincidental.

ISBN 978-93-5954-8876

Printed at Ramprintograph, Delhi

First printing 2026

This reprint edition, April 2026

Book design by Maithili Joshi

—For Norah, my Magic Gem

CHAPTER 1

Lily Willowjal dove headfirst into the sparkling waters of Lake Sapphire. The moment she slipped under the surface, her legs transformed into a beautiful mermaid's tail. It twinkled in shades of dewdrop blue.

Flicking her tail, Lily glided deeper into the water. Her lavender hair, pinned with seashells, floated behind her like a cloud of petals. Lily blinked twice and turned on her aqua-vision powers.

Instantly, the underwater world rippled into focus! The bottom of the lake shimmered with a soft, golden light. Pearly shells of every size peeked out from the sand like hidden treasures. A colorful coral garden swayed in the gentle current. A school of glimmerfish darted through it, flickering like tiny rainbows. They twirled around Lily, calling her to play.

"Not today, glimmerlings," Lily said. Tiny bubbles floated out of her mouth. She itched to join them. But Lily was on a mission.

As a Magic Water Gem, it was her job to help protect all aquatic life in lakes, oceans, and rivers. Plus, with her magic, she could transform into a mermaid whenever she wanted to! But Lily's magic wasn't complete. She hadn't earned any of her gemstones yet.

Every Magic Gem in the land of Elementis needed something special to make their powers stronger—enchanted gemstones. With every gemstone earned, a Gem's magic grew more powerful.

Lily spun on her tail. A string of familiar squeals caught her attention. She grinned and dashed ahead until she spotted a family of glowfur otters splashing near the shallows. Lily watched their little webbed feet, round ears, long, fluffy tails, and soft fur that glowed like a thousand sparklebugs at night!

But her stomach knotted.

"I can do this," she said. Her main job was to perform the glowfur otters' weekly checkups. But things weren't turning out quite as well as she had hoped.

Lily swam up to the surface.

"Heya, friends!" she called out, trying to sound casual. The otters circled her, chirping playfully.

This is my chance! she thought.

As Lily stretched out her hands, the otters realized it was checkup time. In a blur, they scattered in every direction!

"Wait!" Lily shouted, chasing after them. The otters squealed as if they were playing a game of water tag. When she finally caught one of the otters, he wriggled free, jumped on her head, and swung from her hair. The otters and the Magic Gems standing on the shore burst into giggles. Lily wanted to hide underwater. She was totally failing at otter checkups and at being a Water Gem!

As a young Water Gem without any gemstones, Lily's magic was only strong enough to help water blossoms bloom, guide schools of fish, and cast simple spells. Lily dreamed of becoming a Wave Weaver just like her mother, who was brave, powerful, and graceful.

Wave Weavers were Water Gems who had

earned all their gemstones and had the strongest water magic in Elementis. Lily's magic felt small and clumsy in comparison. If she had earned even her first gemstone, she would breeze through the otter checkups without any trouble.

The water around Lily shimmered, and she snapped out of her thoughts. A glittering, turquoise tail fin swished toward her. Lily's eyes widened. It was her mother, Guru Jasmine! She was one of the four Magic Guru Gems on the island.

"I'm here, Lilydew!" her mother called out. Lily wanted to vanish under the waves at the sound of her pet name in *public*! "Need help?" she asked as her long, blue hair slipped elegantly over her shoulder.

Before Lily could stop her, her mother called forth the magic of her gemstones. Swirls of peacock blue, rose red, ivy green, and petal pink flowed out of her shimmery gemstone bangles. They trailed behind her like a sparkling robe as she zipped across the shallows at turbo speed and gathered all the otters.

"Mom, you didn't have to come!" Lily's cheeks burned from having her mother help her in front of all the other Gems.

"There now, glowfur otters can be tricky

little creatures," her mother said, lifting Lily's chin to meet her gaze. A warm kindness shone from her sea-blue eyes. Lily fidgeted with a seashell in her hair. Her mother was always so patient with her. "Come, let me show you again."

Guru Jasmine scooped up an otter. She checked its heart, lungs, and paws and then let it splash back into the water.

"See? I know you can do it."

Lily's heart sank. Her mom made it look so easy. Even though Lily tried her best, she never seemed to get it right. If she had her gemstone, she could make her mother proud and not need any rescuing.

But only the bravest and the most skilled Magic Gems earned their gemstones. Lily knew Gems who had risked their own lives to save another, calmed raging storms to guide schools of lost fish home, and even made vines grow strong and fast to save animals trapped in quicksand.

Unfortunately for Lily, if she was one thing, it was *not* brave. Her list of fears could fill the ocean. As for her skills, she couldn't even get the otters to listen to her!

"Why don't you give it a try?" encouraged Guru Jasmine.

Lily nervously reached for Cotton, a young

albino otter with the cuddliest white fur. To her surprise, Cotton jumped into her arms under Guru Jasmine's gaze. Lily quickly completed the checkup and let him go.

"Good job!" said her mother. She gave Lily a proud pat on the cheek before swimming off to help someone else.

Feeling a splash of courage, Lily tried again. Once again, the otter sprang out of her grip! In a flash, the rest escaped too. Lily flopped back onto the water.

I'm officially the worst Water Gem, she thought miserably.

Lily turned back to the otters, who were busy blowing bubbles at one another. Suddenly, an idea popped into her mind, sending a tingling through her scales.

Will it work? she wondered.

Lily didn't know—but she had to try!

CHAPTER 2

Lily began to blow bubble after bubble. When she was done, she called on her magic. It rushed down her arms and poured out of her fingertips in a waterfall of powder-blue sparkles. Her magic swirled around the bubbles, making them buzz.

The first part of her plan was complete! Next,

she needed to place a message in each of the bubbles.

Are the medicines helping your tummyache, Mr. Belly-Rubs? Lily thought of the papa otter, who loved a good belly rub and had gobbled one too many salty reedclams again.

Pari, how are you and the litter doing? She wondered about the new mama with a fairy-shaped mark on her back. She had given birth to four pups only a month ago.

Once Lily had finished placing messages inside all the bubbles, she let out a breath.

"Time to cast the spell," she said, and then scrunched her nose, thinking of the right words for the spell to work. Finally, she chanted:

"Bobbing bubbles, set sail and explore,

Find the otters you are meant for.

Heartbeats strong, lungs breathing clear,

Let the truth in the bubbles appear.

If all is well, glow clear and blue,

If there's trouble, turn a crimson hue."

Lily gave the bubbles a push, and off they zipped in different directions. Then, with a grin, she slipped underwater.

"Got you!"

Lily locked her arms around Cotton. He nuzzled against her. Seconds later, Twinklepaws,

Dasher, and Tumbles tugged at her fins. Lily couldn't resist! She laughed and chased the otters through the water and sent them flying down the muddy banks.

Before long, the bubbles she'd sent out came floating back. One after the other, they glowed bright and blue. *Mr. Belly-Rubs had forgotten his medicine, but your message reminded him to take it. His lungs are strong!* the bubble reported under Lily's touch. Several others returned carrying more good news.

Lily somersaulted with glee. Her plan had worked! She still needed to check on the otters, but the hardest part was done.

Leaving Cotton, Dasher, Tumbles, and Twinklepaws to see who could make the biggest splashes, Lily dove into the otters' underground dens. After visiting the older otters, she made her way to Pari's burrow.

Where are they? she wondered, peering into the dark tunnels.

Lily looked under mossy rocks, behind sunken logs, and between fields of swaying starstalks. As a Water Gem, she could hold her breath underwater for a long time. But after fifteen minutes of searching, she burst through the surface, gasping for air. There was no sign of Pari or her litter anywhere.

Around her, Magic Gems were busy conducting their own daily checks. Lily found her best friend, Imara flitting above a lumilotus. She was guiding a newly hatched hummingfly to drink nectar from the flower.

The morning sun lit up her delicate wings and pink dress. Imara was an Air Gem. It was her responsibility to protect the weather and all creatures that fly. And the coolest part—she could turn into a sprite as small as Lily's palm!

Lily shot toward her like a dart.

"Is everything okay?" Imara's brows flew up. She changed into her full-size form.

"I can't find Pari or her pups," Lily said.

Imara frowned. "I've been here all morning, and I haven't seen them. Maybe Rio knows?"

Rio was their other best friend. Lily found him climbing up a towering oak tree. As a young Earth Gem, the plants and trees on the island were under his care.

Lily called out, but Rio didn't hear her. He was busy inspecting a broken branch dangling from the trunk. By the time Lily swam to the shore, green sparkles glimmered from Rio's fingers. The branch fused to the trunk, and its drooping leaves sprang to life.

Lily whistled and Rio turned. His mop of messy, forest-green hair fell over his eyes.

"Have you seen Pari and her pups?" shouted Lily.

Rio shaded his eyes with his hand and scanned the lake. "I don't see them anywhere . . ."

If Pari and her pups weren't in the shallows, there was only one place they could be.

The deep.

Where the waters grew dark and colder. Where dangerous creatures lurked. Where even the strongest swimmers could get trapped in currents.

Fear gripped Lily. She had never been that far before.

"You have to be brave," she murmured to herself, taking slow, steady breaths.

Not too far away, sharp squeaks pierced the air. Lily leaped into the water, thinking it was one of the pups. But it was a mama porcupine and her baby clinging to a log floating in the water. The log was their home, and it had fallen into the lake!

Before Lily could help, a roar shook the air. A dragon as large as a mare stomped out of the trees.

"Stop the log!" the dragon yelled. But the

current swept it away before anyone could reach it. The dragon dashed to the shore and, with a quick sweep of its tail, brought the porcupines safely to shore.

"Don't worry, I'll make you a new home," the dragon said to the porcupines, before charging into the trees. A moment later, it returned with a big piece of driftwood. Standing back, the dragon opened its mouth and breathed. A stream of shimmering fire shot out. The flames danced over the wood, carving out a hollow just the right size—big enough for the porcupines, but too small for larger predators. For the finishing touch, the dragon traced a pattern of swirling leaves and flowers onto the driftwood. It glowed in motes of crimson glitter.

With a shake, the dragon transformed into a girl with long tresses of bright red hair. It was Scarlett, a Fire Gem who helped protect creatures that lived on land.

"You'll be safe here," Scarlett said, nudging the porcupines into their new home. The porcupines squealed and scurried inside.

Lily watched in awe. Scarlett never feared a problem. Last month, she had saved a wounded fawn lost in the Shadowleaf Forest, making her the first one in their group to earn a gemstone.

It was a story she told to anyone who would listen.

Lily didn't care about Scarlett's boastfulness. But she wondered if she would ever be brave enough to dive into the deep in the same way Scarlett had set out into the forest alone. The deep, the dark, and the unknown were three of Lily's biggest fears.

"Are you here to admire my powers?" Scarlett asked, twirling her ruby gemstone necklace.

"Huh? No! What?" Lily stuttered. "I—I came to look for Pari and her pups. I thought I heard them, but it was the porcupines."

Scarlett's amber eyes flashed. "You've lost your charges?"

"No! I mean, I don't know . . ." The words tumbled out of Lily's mouth. Before she could say any more, a bubble sped toward her. It glowed red like a flashing siren.

It was Pari's bubble!

Lily placed her hands around the bubble and felt for the message it carried.

Hurry! Pebbles is hurt!

CHAPTER 3

Lily chased after the glowing bubble. Imara's mouth opened like she was about to ask what had happened, but Lily didn't have time to explain. Pebbles, Pari's youngest pup, needed her. *Now.*

The bubble charged ahead, leading Lily out of Lake Sapphire. Waves slapped against one another, and the waters narrowed into a frothing river. Lily grabbed on to the bubble, trying not to panic.

The bubble bounced along, faster and faster. Just when Lily thought they were going to crash into the old shipwreck by the shore, the bubble stopped. A wave splashed into her face.

"Puh—ri? Pah—bules?" Lily shouted, coughing up water and swimming around the broken ship. "Is anyone here?"

A chorus of yelps rose above the choppy waves. Lily darted forward. Behind the hull covered in barnacles, she spotted Pari's fairy-shaped birthmark! The mama otter was frantically swimming in circles.

"Coming through!" Lily said, squeezing past the pups huddling around her.

She gasped. Pebbles was caught in a fishing net!

"Don't worry, I'm going to get you out!" Lily

tugged at the net, trying to loosen it. But the more Pebbles thrashed in terror, the tighter the net became around him.

"Hold still!" pleaded Lily. She pulled harder, and even tried biting the fibers, but the net stayed firmly in place. She needed a new plan, and *fast!*

"I'll be back in a flash, okay?" she promised Pari. The mama otter nodded sorrowfully.

The pups cried loudly as Lily plunged into the water. She turned on her aqua-vision and scanned the depths for anything she could find to cut the net with. Kicking her tail harder, Lily swam toward the riverbed. Finally, her hands brushed against the sand, and her fingers closed on something sharp.

A broken clamshell!

She grabbed it and rushed to the surface. When the pups parted for her, Lily's heart dropped to her tail. Pebbles wasn't moving much. His eyelids drooped.

"LILYYYYYYYY!" voices cried out in the distance.

Lily swiveled to find Imara and Rio paddling toward her in two rowboats.

"What can we do to help?" asked Rio.

If there was time, Lily would have given her best friends the biggest hug. "One of you needs to take the pups home. The other can help me cut the net."

"On it," Imara said, and began herding the pups. "Come on, kiddos!"

Pari stayed behind, her whiskers twitching with worry. She watched as Lily tried to slice the net using the broken edge of the clamshell.

"I don't know if this is going to work," said Lily. Tears filled her eyes as she watched Pebbles growing weaker. Rio's face hardened like it always did when he got serious.

"I have an idea," he said, and jumped onto the shipwreck. Lily heard him picking things up and tossing them aside. Finally, he held up the jagged end of an oar. "This should help!"

Working together, Rio and Lily cut through the fibers at double the speed. At last, the net fell away, and Pebbles sank into Lily's arms. She noticed one of his front paws had a deep gash!

Lily placed a palm over the cut and squeezed her eyes shut. She hoped her magic would work.

"Bleeding cut, mend and seal,

With my magic, repair and heal!"

When she opened her eyes, the gash remained. Pebbles whimpered softly. Lily wished for the millionth time that she had earned her gemstone. But now wasn't the time for wishes.

"Let's hurry back home," she said to Rio.

"I'll follow you," he replied, climbing into his boat. "You're way faster in the water."

Lily nodded. She carefully attached Pebbles to her back using a shawl Imara had brought with her. Then she swam at full speed to Sapphire Shores. Lily hoped they weren't too late.

CHAPTER 4

The four Magic Guru Gems gathered beneath the ancient banyan. Its leaves sparkled like drops of frozen starlight. When they swayed, a tinkling melody drifted in the breeze.

Lily's heart pounded like a pod of storm-whales charging through the seas. Her mother,

Guru Jasmine, had called for an emergency healing ceremony.

“Let us begin,” her mother said, stepping into the lake with a basket in her hands. Inside the basket was Pebbles. He lay snuggled under a blanket of fuzzleaf clovers. His wounded paw stuck out, wrapped in a bandage made from leaves and herbs.

"I'm scared to look," Lily said, peeking through her fingers. Pari, too, whimpered from the shallows.

"Pebbles will be A-OK once the Gurus cast their healing spell," said Imara. Lily nodded, even though she heard a quaver in her best friend's voice.

One by one, the Guru Gems entered the water and placed their hands over Pebbles's bandaged paw.

"Haven't you caused enough trouble already?"

a prickly voice whispered in Lily's ear. She turned to find Scarlett sitting behind them, smirking.

"Otter pups are mischievous and fast, you know!" Imara jumped to Lily's rescue.

"And like most creatures, they hate check-ups. It could've happened to any of us," added Rio.

"Well, it *never* happens to me," Scarlett boasted.

Lily felt a lump in her throat. Scarlett was right. What kind of a Gem loses her charges and lets them get hurt? *Not a very good one . . .* a tiny voice echoed in her head.

"Don't listen to her," Imara said, squeezing

Lily's arm. A shimmering, blue-winged cicawisp landed on Lily, and Imara gently picked it up. The cicawisp glowed golden for a moment, then fluttered straight into Scarlett's mouth.

"Ewww! Blech! Yuck!" Scarlett coughed out the cicawisp in a burst of blue and pink sparks. "Get away from me, you pesky critter!"

As the cicawisp flew away, Lily could've sworn it winked at Imara. Imara gave a sly smile, and Lily and Rio giggled.

Scarlett glared, hot with embarrassment. "If you had a gemstone like I do, you could have asked the otters if they'd seen Pebbles and found him sooner!" She held up her gleaming ruby gemstone necklace as if it were a medal she had won.

Lily held back her tears. *And if I were as brave as Scarlett, I wouldn't have hesitated before swimming out of Sapphire Shores to look for Pebbles,* she thought.

"Pebbles is in good hands." Imara comforted her. "Look, the Gurus are about to cast the spell."

Guru Jasmine's aquamarine scales glinted like jewels under the sun. Lily held her breath. Even the cicawisps stopped chittering.

The Guru Gems chanted:

"A healing touch, the waters weave,

On Pebbles's spirit, young and free.

Mend his wound and soothe the pain,

In water's grace, let his strength regain."

A halo of rainbow glitter rose from the Guru Gems and surrounded Pebbles. When the glitter disappeared, Guru Jasmine returned to shore. Her brow furrowed deeply.

"Pebbles is alive," she announced. "However, the spell did not heal his wound. His life remains in danger."

"No!" Lily's fingers flew to her lips.

"We are left with only one option: to seek the enchanted blossoms of the Great Lunaris."

Gasps echoed through the crowd.

Lily remembered reading about the Great Lunaris in their Petals and Potions class. It said the magical tree's flowers sparkled like pink sapphires and carried the nectar of life. A single petal could save a dying soul.

But no one had traveled to the Great Lunaris in a long, long time.

Guru Jasmine raised her arms to calm the uproar. "The Guru Gems must remain here to care for Pebbles. So we ask the bravest Gems to come forward and bring back the blossoms. To reach the Great Lunaris, you will have to survive the murky marshlands and cross the roaring Dragondrop Waterfall. You will face swift currents and dangers lurking in the waters. But Pebbles needs you."

Lily felt her heart banging against her chest. She was far from the bravest Gem. Her mother had been brave when she was young. Like Scarlett, she was the first one of her class to earn her gemstone, which she proudly wore as a bangle. But Lily wasn't like her mother. She was nervous about trying new things and exploring unknown places.

All she wanted was to stay in Sapphire Shores, taking care of the aquatic plants and animals. But she had messed even that up.

"I—I will go," said Lily. Her voice cracked like a dry riverbed. No matter how afraid she was of the journey, she would never forgive herself if she let her fears put Pebbles's life in more danger. "Pebbles is under my care, and I—I promise to do whatever it takes to bring back the Lunaris blossoms."

"*We* promise," Rio said, standing up beside her. Imara jumped to her feet too.

"You both will come?" Lily asked, her voice full of surprise. She was scared to go alone, but she didn't want her friends to risk their lives for her.

"Of course! What are friends for?" Imara grinned. "Besides, we'd do anything for Pebbles."

A wave of happiness washed over Lily. She truly had the best friends in all the waters!

"Scarlett, would you like to join them too?" asked Guru Jasmine. "Together, the four of you will represent the healing powers of all the Magic Gems."

"I would love to join my friends, Guru Jasmine," Scarlett replied with syrupy sweetness. "With the powers of my gemstone, I can help us face the dangers together and reach the Lunaris faster."

Lily, Imara, and Rio exchanged glances. Scarlett was definitely up to something. For one, she had never called them her "friends" before. But, of course, her mother fell for her act.

Guru Jasmine smiled. "I am proud to see Gems supporting one another." Then her expression turned grim. "Pay heed, the flowers of the Lunaris bloom only under moonlight and must be harvested before the first ray of sunlight. Remember to swim north, and whatever you do, stay clear of the Inky Lagoon. Its mystical waters can trick even the most seasoned travelers."

Lily's eyes grew as wide as clamshells. She didn't know what worried her more: Scarlett's sudden desire to be friends or the dangers of the Inky Lagoon.

CHAPTER 5

"I want you to have this."

Guru Jasmine placed a compass, hanging from a chain, around Lily's neck. The compass had a silver dial with beautiful carvings of waves, fish, and mermaids.

"But it's a family heirloom! Grandma gave it to you. What if I lose it?" Lily asked.

Guru Jasmine rested her hand on Lily's shoulder. "It's a special compass, Lilydew. Trust in it, and it will be your guiding light."

"Almost forgot!" Lily's dad called out as he wiggled through the crowd that had gathered to say goodbye to the Magic Gems. "You and your friends can use my bread baskets to carry the Lunaris blossoms!"

Her dad was the best baker on the island and her biggest cheerleader. He handed Lily a stack of four baskets. Each had a lid and was strung onto a glimmervine. Lily slipped them over her shoulder.

Her dad kneeled beside her. "Now don't you

forget, everything you need for this journey is within you." Lily nodded, trying to swallow the lump forming in her throat. "And hurry back soon. I'll have your favorite fernfluff pancakes waiting for you!"

"Thanks, Dad." She wrapped him in a tight hug and breathed in the sweet scent of freshly baked lotus bread surrounding him.

"Lily, let's go!" Scarlett hollered from a large boat. She, Rio, and Imara were sitting inside waiting for her. Lily saw the words *Anchorheart* painted along the side of the hull.

"The *Anchorheart* will keep you safe," Guru Jasmine said to Lily and her friends. "The

Guru Gems and I have enchanted the boat to be anchored to each of you. No matter what happens, it will find you."

Lily glanced at Imara and Rio. That meant the journey ahead was dangerous enough that losing the boat was a possibility!

"Safe tidings, young Gems!" the crowd chanted as Lily gave her parents a final hug and swam up to the boat. Pari, her pups, and the other otters brushed up against her, saying their goodbyes too. Cotton yipped, scampering around Lily.

"I know you want to help, but I need you to stay here and look after Pebbles." She looked into his big, puddle-brown eyes and kissed the top of his furry head.

Lily turned toward Pari. "I promise to be back as soon as I can."

Pari nuzzled her cheek before letting Lily go.

The afternoon sun blazed above the four Gems sailing across the glittering waters. Lily glanced over her shoulder. Sapphire Shores was now smaller than the size of her thumb.

"I think it's best if you all follow my lead," declared Scarlett.

"If anyone should lead us, it's Lily," protested Rio. "Pebbles is under her care, *and* she has the compass."

"But I have a gemstone!" Scarlett said.

"So? Having your gem doesn't make you better than us," Imara replied, her face turning red.

"Everyone, take a breath!" said Lily. "We're a team. What matters is getting to the Lunaris and not wasting time. So, if you want to lead, Scarlett, go ahead."

Scarlett flashed a toothy grin and stuck out her hand. "Great decision! Now, hand me your compass."

Lily touched her neck. "My compass?"

An uneasy feeling crept over her as Scarlett nodded. She didn't want to part with her grandma's compass. But she also didn't want to start a fight.

"Please be careful with it," she said, handing the compass to Scarlett. From the corner of

her eye, Lily saw Rio and Imara shaking their heads.

Once Scarlett wore the compass around her neck, they all huddled around it.

"Isn't the needle supposed to stop spinning?" asked Rio.

"It is." Imara frowned. "A compass's needle

is made of metal. So, it should *always* show us which way is north. I don't understand why this needle won't stop turning."

The Gems aimed the compass in every direction. They shook it. But the needle kept circling.

"Great, it's broken," Scarlett said, blowing a crimson strand away from her face. "I guess we pick a direction and hope it's north?"

"Let me try," said Lily. There was no way her mother would have given her a broken compass.

Scarlett hesitated but then agreed. Lily held the compass in her palm. She traced her fingers over the little shells and shimmerstones. Her mother had called it a "*special* compass."

"Trust in it, and it will be your guiding light," she had said.

I know you're not broken. Please show us which way is north, Lily asked silently.

The arrow didn't stop spinning. But the compass buzzed softly. Like it was alive! Lily held back her excitement. Was she supposed to *ask* the compass for directions? Was that the secret to making it work?

She closed her eyes and tried again.

Can you please guide us to the Great Lunaris?

A ripple, smooth as velvet, spread through

her as an image of an enormous tree glittering in pink flowers appeared in her mind.

"It stopped spinning!" Imara squealed.

Lily opened her eyes. The arrow was pointing north!

CHAPTER 6

An hour passed. The water around the Magic Gems stretched out endlessly on all sides.

"Where in the name of Elementis is the Lunaris?" exclaimed Scarlett. The sun dipped low, painting ribbons of pink across the horizon. Lily didn't need a watch to know that time was slipping by. "At this rate, we'll never find it in time! I'm going to ask the compass again."

Scarlett opened the compass and closed her eyes. As the needle began to slow, a look of fear flashed across her face.

"What's wrong?" asked Imara.

Before Scarlett could answer, her body began to shudder. With a loud crackle, she grew larger and larger, transforming into her dragon self. Lily, Imara, and Rio screamed as Scarlett's fire-rimmed tail whipped through the air. The *Anchorheart* rocked wildly, and the Gems toppled over.

Scarlett crashed into the water with a massive splash. A huge wave rose. It towered high above the Gems, trapping them like fish caught on a hook.

BOOM!

The wave came crashing down. Lily plunged into the icy water, her legs instantly transforming into a glittery tail. As she kicked her tail, trying to swim up to the surface, a powerful current held her down. Water rushed up her nose and into her mouth. Her lungs burned, struggling for breath.

At once, Lily realized the wave had created a riptide! She was sure of it because she had given a presentation on riptides in their Survival in the Swells class just last month. Not too far away, she spotted green and pink shapes somersaulting in the water. Imara and Rio were trapped too!

Lily's chest tightened. If she and her friends didn't escape the riptide, they were going to drown! But with every stroke Lily took, the tide was dragging her back in. As she waved her arms furiously, she tried to remember what to do.

First: Don't panic and don't fight against the current. Then swim parallel to the current and start to angle yourself toward the shore.

Lily took a deep breath and swam sideways, keeping the shoreline in sight. Finally, she could feel herself breaking free of the current!

Lily locked eyes with Imara and Rio and waved for them to follow. But they weren't strong swimmers like her. They were getting pulled deeper into the water!

I have to go back in and save them! she thought. Calling what little strength she had left, Lily dove back into the current. With each stroke, her energy faded fast.

Can't. Give. Up. Have. To. Help. Rio. And. Imara. Her lungs ached, and her arms slowed.

Right then, a glowing orb zipped past her. It dashed toward her friends, darting to and fro like a moonbeam chasing the waves.

Lily couldn't believe her eyes. It was Cotton!

In a flurry of quick spins, Cotton nudged Imara and Rio with his nose and guided them toward Lily. As they got closer, Lily grabbed each of her friends' arms, and together they swam away from the tide.

"We did it!" Lily exclaimed, spitting out a fountain of water. The tide had brought them to a quiet, narrow stream.

"Thanks to this little guy!" Rio said, turning to the dome of white fur hiding beneath the surface. Cotton gurgled and swirled around them. Lily hugged him tightly.

"How did you get here?"

Cotton bounded out of her arms and leaped into the water. He skimmed the surface until he hopped onto the *Anchorheart* a few meters away. Lily turned to her friends, her eyes wide. The *Anchorheart* had found them, just like her mother had said! After they climbed back into the boat, Cotton stuck his head out of Lily's basket.

She laughed, ruffling his fur. "Is that where you were hiding this whole time?"

Cotton nodded with a big grin.

"Attaboy!" Rio fist-bumped Cotton's paw. "You saved my life. All of you did."

"Not all of us. Scarlett's gone," Imara said, turning serious.

Lily looked around. Apart from a dead tree that split the stream into two creeks, they were completely alone. Scarlett had vanished. Lily reached for the compass around her neck, but her fingers found nothing.

"This couldn't have been Scarlett's plan all along, could it?" she asked. Was she foolish to have trusted Scarlett with the compass?

"What do you mean?" asked Rio.

"Scarlett distracted us with a tidal wave and stole the compass so she could return with the flowers and save Pebbles's life all by herself," answered Imara.

"Would Scarlett really do that?" Rio's usually brave voice trembled. "Would she leave us stranded here?"

Lily didn't want to believe that Scarlett would abandon them like this. She could be boastful and a little full of herself, but she'd seen Scarlett

be the first one to help when someone was hurt or in trouble.

The waters lapped around the bark of the rotting tree as Lily stared at the two possible paths ahead. Without the compass, they had no idea which way to go. Both paths looked the same. Each was lined with soaring trees, dark foliage, and wild sweetgrass. Cotton paddled toward the dead tree. He looked worried too. The sky darkened to a deep shade of lavender as Lily faced her best friends.

"As long as it's the three of us, I'm not afraid," she said.

"You're right." Imara slipped an arm around Rio and Lily. "We can do this."

Rio nodded, his face brightening. "All right, which way then, Captains?"

"How about we try Spin the Boat?" Lily suggested. It was a game they played as kids when they wanted to decide who would go first—in this case, which path they should take.

"Spin us, Cotton!" said Imara. As Cotton gave the prow of the boat a good push, the Gems closed their eyes and pointed ahead. The boat spun in place. Slowly, it came to a stop. When they opened their eyes, the Gems saw the path their hands pointed toward.

"And off we go," said Rio.

As they sailed down the creek to the left, Lily wondered if they had made the right choice.

CHAPTER 7

The *Anchorheart* glided smoothly through the peaceful water. Tall blades of sweetgrass danced by the shore, filling the air with the scent of sugar puffs. Lily's stomach let out a loud rumble. They had skipped lunch, and she wished she could pluck a blade and suck on its candy sweetness! Above her, gold, speckled butterflies fluttered their wings while bobble-toads hopped from reed to reed.

It was picture perfect.

Until . . .

A shadow fell over them. Lily gulped. It was as if someone had pulled a curtain over the sun. Within seconds, the early evening sky had turned into a dark, swampy twilight!

Imara scrunched up her nose. "Something smells gross . . ."

Lily shuddered as the water suddenly grew marshy and thick with weeds. Thorny vines with rotting flowers dangled from crooked branches. A dark squiggle spun past her. Cotton yelped and leaped into her lap.

Another squiggle appeared. Then another. Each one got longer, thicker, and smellier.

The streaks looked just like—

Lily's heart pounded in her mouth.

Ink.

"Um . . . I think we have a problem," she said quietly.

Rio's gaze fell on the squiggles. "A very big problem!" he cried out.

Imara's eyes doubled in size at the stinky streaks. "We're in the Inky Lagoon!" she exclaimed.

Lily was too scared to speak. Gone were the golden butterflies, the leaping toads, and the sugary wild grass. In their place, unseen creatures hissed from the shadowy banks and scurried up the dead, skeletal trees.

Stay calm, stay calm, the voice in her head

chanted. Lily added *sailing through the creepy darkness* to her growing list of fears.

"C-c-couldn't this be the murky marshlands Guru Jasmine told us we would have to cross?" Rio stuttered in a rush. "It could mean we're on the right path . . ."

Lily shook her head. Nothing about this place felt or smelled right.

"We need to go back," she said. As they turned to leave, a misty fog rolled in. Lily rubbed her eyes. She could barely see two feet in front of her!

"Wait, I hear something," Rio said, raising his hand to stop Lily from turning the *Anchorheart* around.

In the distance, a girl's voice sang in a haunting tune. "Come hither, come, come to me."

Rio grabbed the steering wheel from Lily and plowed the *Anchorheart* through the dark waters. "We can't leave! She needs our help!"

"Hold on!" shouted Lily. "Didn't my mom say that the mystical waters of the Inky Lagoon could trick us?"

She turned to Imara for help, but Imara had a dazed look on her face too.

"We should help the poor girl," she said as tears ran down her face.

"Please, let's think for a minute. This could be a trap," Lily said desperately. But Imara stood beside Rio. They stared into the foggy darkness.

The hypnotic voice filled the lagoon again. As much as Lily wanted to ignore it, she felt her senses growing dull. Her arms began to move like a puppet being controlled by somebody else. Silently, she joined Imara and Rio.

The *Anchorheart* arrived at a large, gray rock jutting out from the shore and over the water. A young girl slid out into the misty twilight. Her skin shone purply blue like a bruise.

Lily, Imara, and Rio snapped out of their trance.

"Don't be scared. I won't harm you," the girl

said. Lily noticed the girl's fingernails were long and curved like a hawk's talons. She inched closer to Rio and Imara, sticking to them like glue.

"Won't you please stay a minute?" the girl pleaded. Her hair, tangled with stones and lakeweed, fell over her dirt-smudged shoulders.

Rio glanced at the near-black sky and covered his nose from the stench of the stinky water. "We don't have time . . . We're in a hurry."

Lily and Imara nodded in agreement.

"Oh, please do reconsider. I won't keep you

long. I rarely meet travelers who come this way . . ."

Lily glanced at her friends. Though she was terrified (and they *were* in a hurry), she sensed a pain in the girl's voice. Lily felt bad.

"We can stay for a minute," she said.

"Simply splendid!" the girl cheered. "I'm Himeropa. That's Greek for 'the lovely voice,'" she said as she slithered forward. "I've never made so many friends in a single day! What are your names?"

As Imara and Rio introduced themselves, Lily noticed Himeropa had a mermaid's tail, just like hers. But Himeropa's lay limply behind her, several of the scales ripped and torn.

"And you are?" Himeropa batted her long-lashed eyes at Lily.

"I—I'm Lily. Are you—a mermaid siren?"

"Sure am. I guard this beautiful oasisss," she crooned. A shiver slid down Lily's back. This place was anything but an oasis. "You see, this is my lagoon, and I protect it from trespassers."

"W-we're not trespassing, promise!" Rio said hurriedly.

"We got lost." Imara's voice quavered.

"Of course, I know that!" A smile spread across Himeropa's face as she propped her chin on her palm. "I have an idea. I'll be right back!"

Himeropa disappeared behind her rock. A few seconds later, she appeared carrying a tray with a teapot and four teacups.

"How about we celebrate with a tea party before you . . . um . . . continue with your travels?"

The Gems turned to each other in panic. They definitely did not have time for a tea party.

Before Lily could politely say no, Himeropa began to sing. Lily's eyes closed, enjoying the sweet harmony.

"That was beautiful," Rio said with a dopey smile on his face.

"Surely, a cup of tea won't delay us too long, right?" Imara asked Lily and Rio. Lily's mind felt light as a feather. Tea sounded wonderful to her.

"We'd love to," she agreed groggily. "We've been traveling for a long time." As if on cue, her stomach let out another rumble, and everyone giggled.

Lily jumped out of the boat and into the river. She didn't care about the smelly, inky water anymore. Imara and Rio followed behind. As they swam up to Himeropa, a sound came from somewhere behind a crooked knot of trees.

But the Magic Gems didn't stop. They kept swimming, eager for tea and a chat. They had nearly made it to shore when the sound erupted again. Lily's scales prickled. The sound seemed an awful lot like a *scream*. A scream from someone she knew!

Lily snapped out of Himeropa's trance and heard the cries again.

"Somebody help me!!"

Her jaw dropped to the riverbed.

The scream belonged to Scarlett!

CHAPTER 8

"Don't move!" Himeropa hissed, flashing a hidden row of sharp, jagged teeth. The Gems startled and broke out of their spells. Himeropa looked terrifying!

"That's our friend, Scarlett!" Lily exclaimed.

"Where is she?" demanded Imara. The Gems hurriedly swam in every direction searching for Scarlett. It didn't matter that she had abandoned them earlier. They were Magic Gems and would stop at nothing to help one of their own.

"I'm going to get the *Anchorheart* so we can escape. You guys keep looking for Scarlett," whispered Rio.

Lily nodded and recited the Magic Gems' motto: "When trouble calls, we rise as one."

"Magic Gems, our work is never done!" Rio and Imara said, completing the motto together.

"Stop! Where are you going?" Himeropa shrieked when she saw Rio swimming toward the *Anchorheart*. When Rio didn't answer, she waved her hand. The *Anchorheart* exploded into pieces. Lily gasped. Himeropa had destroyed their only means of escape!

"I forbid you to leave!" Himeropa yelled.

"But—" began Lily.

As Himeropa's anger rose, the river water began to spin like a whirlpool. Lily, Rio, and Imara desperately tried to keep their heads above the churning waters. Slowly, a cage of twisted vines and gnarly roots rose from the depths, wrapping around each of them. The Magic Gems were trapped!

Himeropa waved her arms again. This time a cage just like theirs floated out from behind the trees. Inside was Scarlett!

"Lily, Rio, Imara! Help me!" she cried, banging on the root-vine bars.

"Silence!" Himeropa ordered as Scarlett's cage fell beside the Gems with a splash. Scarlett quieted, her lips trembling. When she saw Lily and her friends were trapped too, her face fell.

"Please, Himeropa, you have to let us out!"

Lily begged. "We haven't done anything wrong!"

The mermaid siren twisted her neck to face Lily. "Do you know your 'friend' stomped through my idyllic lagoon with her big dragon feet and sent a stream of fire toward me? Luckily for me, siren magic blocks Gem magic. So, she was forced to return to her human form."

Lily glanced at Scarlett, who lowered her gaze to her feet.

"When *she* entered my lagoon, I knew I smelled something fishy. And not the delicious kind," added Himeropa. "My siren magic warned me that she was a thief. Once I trapped her, she confessed that a compass had brought her to the lagoon. And that the compass didn't even belong to her!"

"I didn't steal the compass!" said Scarlett. "At least I didn't mean to . . ." Her voice grew small. She turned to Lily, Imara, and Rio. "When we were on the boat and I asked the compass to show me the way to the Great Lunaris, an image of her and this terrible place flashed in my mind. I got so scared, my dragon form took over. Before I knew it, I was wading through these waters. I thought if I could scare her off, she wouldn't be able to hurt us with her evil ways." Tears brimmed in Scarlett's deep-crimson eyes.

Himeropa's nostrils flared.

"Excuse me, I—I'm *not* evil!" she sputtered. "You didn't even speak to me before trying to hurt me." Himeropa wiped away a glistening teardrop. "Why does everyone want to hurt me?"

"Not everyone. We don't want to hurt you," said Rio.

"That's what everybody says . . ." Himeropa's gaze drifted into the distance. "Once, centuries ago, I met a sailor. I thought he was my friend. He promised we would explore all the lands of Elementis together. Alas, when it was time to leave, he betrayed me and wounded me with his spear. I lost my heart and my freedom in one day." Himeropa glanced at her ripped scales and lifeless tail.

A pang of sadness hit Lily. She couldn't imagine having her tail destroyed and never being able to swim again.

"These days, anyone who lays eyes on me thinks I want to harm them. But that is far from the truth. I only take revenge if someone lies or tries to hurt me. So, when your friend swam through my lagoon trying to scare me with dragon fire, I had to teach her a lesson. I trapped her and decided she'll be my dinner later." Himeropa flicked her tongue over her cold, blue lips.

"DINNER?!" yelped the Gems. Lily turned to Rio and Imara. They couldn't let Scarlett be eaten!

"I made a mistake!" cried Scarlett. "I shouldn't have tried to hurt you!"

"Too late!" Himeropa settled into a comfortable position. "Now isn't this lovely? Being together and having a chat?" She lifted the teapot and began pouring tea into the teacups. "It can get pretty lonely here sometimes . . ." she said. "I haven't had a conversation in years."

A glowslug crawled out of its underwater

burrow, and the reflection of the moon rippled in the water. Nighttime had arrived. They needed to leave! But Lily could tell Himeropa liked to talk. She probably would too if she hadn't spoken to someone in such a long time.

"I'm sorry you've been hurt and lonely for so long," said Lily. She hoped what she was going to say next wouldn't send Himeropa into a fit of rage. "The reason why we've traveled to your lagoon is because we are on our way to the Great Lunaris. Back in Sapphire Shores, Pebbles, a baby otter, is sick and needs our help. If we don't return with the Lunaris flowers by sunrise, he won't heal in time."

"Oh." Himeropa's voice softened. "I once had a pet otter . . ." She glanced at Cotton, who immediately ducked out of sight. "Well, if I let you go, do you promise to return this way once you've collected the blossoms?"

"We do!" the Gems shouted together.

"But *you*, I'm keeping." Himeropa pointed a curved finger at Scarlett.

Scarlett threw the Gems a desperate look.

"We won't leave without Scarlett," insisted Imara. "She shouldn't have tried to hurt you, but she was scared. Deep down, Scarlett has a good heart."

"But if I let you all go, I'll be alone again . . ."

"If you let us go, we will *all* come back to visit you," reasoned Lily. "Friendship is based on kindness and trust. If you let us go, we'll *want* to be your friend."

Himeropa shifted in her spot. She bit her frost-blue lip, deep in thought. After a minute, she slithered closer. "If you want me to believe your promise, then answer this riddle, and I will do as you say."

The four of them leaned forward as Himeropa sang.

"I cannot be bent, twisted, or sold,

Yet I'm worth more than silver or gold.

Hidden in darkness, I shine the light,

Without me, wrong looks right.

I can't be broken, though many may try,

What am I, that no one can deny?"

"Guesses, anyone?" asked Imara. Her gaze ping-ponged among Lily's, Rio's, and Scarlett's cages.

"Could it be a diamond?" Rio said eagerly. "Or a key?"

"Maybe a compass?" added Imara.

Lily shook her head. "Each of them can be bent, twisted, and sold. What about oxygen? It's definitely more valuable than silver or gold!"

"Don't think so. It's hard to 'break' oxygen." Imara frowned.

Cotton nuzzled between their cages, trying to bite through the bars. But the bars didn't budge. When he tried again at Scarlett's cage, she buried her nose in his wet fur.

"Don't look at me . . ." she said. "I . . . I've never been good at puzzles or riddles." Tears glimmered in her eyes.

Lily held Scarlett's hand. "Don't worry. We're going to get out."

As Imara and Rio tossed guesses back and forth, Lily thought about the story Himeropa had told them. The answer to her riddle had to be more obvious than random guesses. The voice in Lily's head told her it was something Himeropa cared about.

But *what*?

Lily turned to the mermaid siren sitting on her rock. She expected to see a look that said, *Ha! I've trapped you all!* Instead, she saw a lonely girl. All Himeropa wanted was to not be alone anymore.

Like a spark in the dark, Lily had the answer! She swung her cage toward Himeropa.

"I know! The answer to your riddle is 'the truth'!"

A smile peeked from Himeropa's lips.

"You've passed my test!" She clapped gleefully. "Only those of true heart and mind can solve the riddle. You did well, Lily. I believe in your promise to return."

She waved her hand, and the cages snapped open. The Magic Gems were free at last!

CHAPTER 9

There was a problem. The Gems had no boat to sail to the Great Lunaris.

"Worry not, friends," Himeropa said in a soothing hum. "Wait, I *am* your friend, right?"

The siren's glowing eyes bore into them, and the four Gems nodded as quickly as they could.

"Stupendous! As your friend, I shall help you

get to the Lunaris with a splash of siren magic!"

As Himeropa sang, the dark waters rose. When she finished, the stars glistened over four ink-water boats bobbing in the lagoon. Each Gem quickly climbed into a boat. Lily was hesitant at first. But when she sat inside, she was surprised to find that a boat made entirely of water could be so sturdy.

Himeropa looked sad as the Gems waved goodbye. But she kept her promise. As she hummed again, the boats lifted onto the crest of a dark and foamy wave.

With a *whoosh,* the Gems zipped out of the Inky Lagoon. They flew past a meadow of whistling flowers, ducked through tunnels of jeweled crystal caves, and soared above a valley of floating islands before landing onto a river with a loud splash.

"We made it!" Scarlett's voice cut through a thunderous crash of water pounding in Lily's ears. Lily looked around. They had arrived at the Dragondrop Waterfall!

Just as hope filled her heart again, the moonlight cast a frightening glow over a *hundred-foot* drop! Lily's happiness faded as quickly as the boat began to pick up speed. Strong winds whipped the hair around her face, and she grabbed on to the sides of the boat.

"Hold on tiiiiiiiiiight!" she yelled, before a wall of mist swallowed her.

Lily nose-dived over the edge of the Dragondrop Waterfall. Between screams, she gulped in a giant breath just before falling sharply into the water. When she rose up to the surface at the foot of the falls, the ink-water boats had vanished.

And so had her friends!

"Over here!!!" Imara called out.

Lily swished her tail and flipped around, but she couldn't see Imara.

"IMARA? RIO? SCARLETT? WHERE ARE YOU ALL??"

A strong breeze rushed past Lily, and a flash of golden glitter swayed toward her.

"I'm heeeeeeerrrre!" Lily heard Imara's tiny voice and felt a smack against her cheek.

"Ouch!" Imara said, plopping onto Lily's shoulder. "That breeze was strong!"

"There you are!" Lily said, patting the soggy sprite. Imara jumped off and turned back into her human form. "Where are the others?"

At that very moment, Cotton, Rio, and Scarlett stuck their heads out of the water.

Lily sighed in relief. They were all safe.

"We made it!" Imara yelled, and they high-fived one another.

"And look!" Rio pointed ahead to a small island shimmering under a blanket of stars. In its center stood the Great Lunaris.

The Magic Gems swam as quickly as they could and scrambled up the shore. The island was unlike anything Lily had ever seen. It was alive with tall trees and strange plants that looked like they had been dipped in glow-in-the-dark paint. Dewdrops from every branch and leaf twinkled like strings of floating fairy lights.

But most magnificent of all was the Lunaris. The Gems craned their necks up at the glitter speckled trunk towering high into the sky. At the top, an explosion of bright pink flowers spilled over a crown of branches. Their petals glowed in a rosy shimmer.

"The Great Bloodrose Lunaris," Lily whispered. "The Tree of Life."

Scarlett tilted her head all the way back.

"Just one problem. How are we going to get up there?"

She had a point. The lowest branches were at least seven feet high!

"Let me try," Imara said, shrinking down to sprite size. Her pearly wings buzzed, and she flitted up the tree.

"Whoa! It's too high," she squeaked as the wind tossed her about like a leaf in a storm. "My wings aren't as strong without a gemstone." Imara flew back down dejectedly.

"Don't worry. Earth Gems are experts at climbing trees," said Rio. He wrapped each leg around the trunk and locked his ankles together.

"You look like you're giving the tree a hug!" Imara giggled.

"*Urgh! Uff!* The bark is too smooth," Rio cried out as he tried shimmying up the trunk. "My foot keeps slippiiiiiing!"

And with that, he fell to the ground with a *thud*.

"Ow." He rubbed his bottom.

"We can't have come this far only to fail!" Scarlett threw her hands up. "Soon it will be dawn, and the blossoms will die!"

Lily paced back and forth. There had to be a way. They were so close to saving Pebbles.

"*We believe in you,*" her mother's voice

whispered through her thoughts. Lily's heart clenched. She couldn't let Pebbles, Pari, and all of Sapphire Shores down.

But out of the water, Lily was beginning to feel helpless. However, when she looked at her friends, she believed in them. Lily realized she wasn't ready to give up yet. As she held on to the last strand of hope, she caught a pair of glowing eyes staring at her. The creature instantly dashed behind a tree and into its burrow.

That's it!

Lily rushed to her friends.

"I believe in you! I believe in us!" she said a little too excitedly.

"Huh?" The Gems looked confused.

"This journey has taught me that we are stronger *together* than we are by ourselves," said Lily. "I would have never made it to the Lunaris if I was alone."

"I wouldn't be here if you hadn't pulled me out of the riptide," Rio said, glancing at Lily, Imara, and Cotton.

Scarlett cleared her throat.

"I would be siren dinner if it hadn't been for the three of you," she murmured. "Lily, I should have never taken your compass." She removed the compass from her neck and returned it to Lily. "Wh-when I got my first gemstone, I thought my powers made me better and stronger than all of you. But I was wrong. Now I know it's *how* you use your powers that makes you a better person. Like how each of you use your magic to help one another and not pull anyone down."

Lily, Rio, and Imara knew it was hard for Scarlett to talk about her feelings when she liked to appear strong.

"I hope you'll forgive me," she said.

"Of course we do," said Lily.

"Friends?"

"Friends!" The Gems giggled and shook on it.

Scarlett turned to Lily. "So, how do we get the flowers?"

"By working together!" Lily answered. "Rio, there are creatures hiding underground. With your ability to talk to burrowing animals, can you ask if they can climb up to the blossoms?"

"Great idea!" replied Rio. He ran to the tree where Lily had spotted the creature and got down on all fours. A glow emanated from him as he transformed into a majestic unicorn. His spiraled horn glimmered in shades of emerald green, and his mane and tail swayed like soft, flowing grass.

As Rio clomped around, pairs of glowing

eyes popped out from the ground. He neighed, sending a string of glitter-green swirls toward them. The long-tailed creatures climbed out of their burrows and gathered around Rio. They chittered excitedly.

"The mudmunks have agreed to help!" Rio said, turning back into himself. "They say if we pluck the flowers from the Great Lunaris, they will wilt immediately and be useless. But if they fall to the ground, the mudmunks can help us gather them up!"

"The Lunaris blossoms have delicate stems. With a few shakes, they should fall to the ground!" said Lily.

"That still doesn't solve how we get to the top." Scarlett frowned.

"Easy. With your help!" exclaimed Imara.

Scarlett's eyes lit up like a Christmas tree, understanding what Imara meant. At once, she morphed into a dragon. At her new size, she came halfway up the trunk of the Lunaris. Tilting her head, she gestured for Lily and Imara to climb up.

Pale streaks of blue began to lighten the dark sky. *It won't be long before the sun comes up and the flowers wilt,* Lily thought as she quickly scrambled onto Scarlett's back while Imara carefully balanced on top of her. Using their

shoulders as foot holds, Rio climbed up to the lowest branches with ease.

On the count of three, he shook the branches.

A sprinkling of pink blossoms twirled gently to the ground like falling snow.

The mudmunks squealed in delight. Scurrying left and right, they used their limbs and tails to scoop up the flowers. Cotton helped too. He dashed to and fro, collecting flowers in his paws and mouth. Soon, the baskets were filled to the brim.

"We did it!" the girls rejoiced, and called for Rio to come back down.

But as soon as he looped his leg around the trunk, his grip slipped, and he fell with a bone-cracking *crash*. Clutching his twisted foot, Rio let out a bloodcurdling scream.

Lily and Imara rushed to his side.

"Step aside!" instructed Scarlett. With calm focus, she felt around Rio's ankle. He twitched and yelped as she prodded the swollen parts.

"You have to be still, okay?"

Rio nodded nervously. Scarlett held her ruby gemstone necklace. As it began to glow, she folded her fingers around his ankle and recited:

"By roots that mend and branches that bend,
I call upon your gentle hand,
Through leaf and dew, through moon and light,
Heal the bone and set it right."

A ribbon of sunset-red sparkles spun around Rio's foot as Scarlett quickly snapped it into place.

"There, you should be able to move it now."

Rio wiggled his foot. It had healed

completely! He leaped and wrapped Scarlett in a big hug.

"That was *so* cool! I hope I earn my first gemstone one day."

"You will. You are all pretty amazing Gems." Scarlett grinned.

"Hey, look what's back!" Imara said, running to the shore.

The *Anchorheart* had returned in one piece!

"Just in time," Lily said, glancing at the brightening sky. Cotton bounded toward her. He squealed, tugging at her feet.

"Down, boy!" She laughed. "Yes, we're heading home to Pebbles!"

But Cotton scampered back to the Lunaris. Lily wondered where he was going. She chased after him until she stopped in disbelief.

A glistening sapphire floated behind the tree.

Lily's heart pounded. Could it really be hers? As she reached out, a surge of magic rippled through her skin like fireworks bursting beneath her fingertips. The gemstone drifted into her palm, light as a falling petal.

Rio and Imara whooped and threw their arms around her. "You earned your first gemstone!"

"Congratulations!" Scarlett beamed. "We never would have reached the Lunaris or

collected the blossoms without you saving us from Himeropa and encouraging us to work together!"

Lily blushed as they hugged and cheered. The Gems then thanked the Great Lunaris and the mudmunks and climbed into the *Anchorheart*. As they tucked their baskets safely on board, Cotton leaped in and snuggled beside Lily.

The time had come to go home to Pebbles.

But first, Lily had a promise to keep.

"To the Inky Lagoon," she whispered to her compass.

CHAPTER 10

Himeropa was lounging lazily on her rock when Lily and her friends arrived. Before they could even greet her, the mermaid siren squealed.

"You came!" she said, flashing her sharp teeth.

"We promised, didn't we?" Lily grinned. *Wasn't it funny,* she thought, *how once you got to know someone, they didn't seem as scary anymore?*

"And your boat found you! I hoped its magic would still work after I fixed it. Sorry about destroying it earlier . . ."

"You mended it and that's all that matters," said Lily. "Also, we brought you something." She nodded to Cotton, who promptly dropped a paw full of Lunaris blooms on Himeropa's rock.

"To heal your tail," explained Imara.

As Himeropa stared at the flowers, blobs of tears rolled down her purply-blue cheeks.

"No one's ever cared for me like this. You *are* my friends!"

The Gems rushed to help Himeropa crush up the Lunaris blooms. When they sprinkled them over her lifeless tail, a puff of pink shimmer swirled over it. Slowly, the torn scales healed before their eyes, turning bright and glossy again.

"I can't believe it!" Himeropa exclaimed. She leaped into the water, flicking her tail and splashing her new friends. As she swam and laughed, the murky waters began to clear. The twisted vines unfurled into soft tendrils. The once-dying trees burst into bloom, and the inky black streaks faded away.

The lagoon sparkled blue.

“My heart is happy again!” Himeropa beamed with the biggest smile on her face.

Lily, Imara, Rio, and Scarlett promised to visit Himeropa next week and pointed their boat toward home.

As they sailed into Sapphire Shores, the blush of dawn peeked over a row of tents lining the water. Lily's parents, along with the other families, had camped out, waiting for the Magic Gems to return. They cheered in relief when Lily, Imara, Rio, and Scarlett sailed to the shore.

Wasting no time, the Gems rushed toward Pebbles. He was in his basket beside a bonfire. Pari and her pups huddled around him. Pebbles's eyes were closed. He looked like he was fast asleep.

The Guru Gems got to work, crushing and spreading the Lunaris blooms over Pebbles's wound. As they entered the water to begin the healing ceremony, Lily stopped her mom.

"Can I help heal Pebbles too?" she asked, holding up her sapphire gemstone. Guru Jasmine's eyes shone with tears.

"Oh, Lilydew, I'm so proud of you!"

Lily joined the Guru Gems in the water and placed her palm on Pebbles's paw. Together, they chanted the healing spell. Slowly, a dome of water rose over them. Lily felt her new Water Gem powers colliding with the magic of the Guru Gems and the Lunaris blooms in a dazzling shower of rainbow glitter. She watched in awe as Pebbles gently lifted into the air.

Lily's scales tingled as the magic of the

flowers washed over her, soft and comforting. It felt like the warmest hug. The softest ripple. Not long after, the glitter disappeared, and the water dropped into the lake. Pebbles floated back into his basket, wrapped in a swirl of sparkles.

"Pebbles's wound is deep. The medicine needs time," said Guru Jasmine. She placed Pebbles near the fire again.

Lily worried if the Lunaris blooms, along with her boosted powers, would be enough to heal him. As they waited for Pebbles, Lily's dad handed out plates of fernfluff pancakes.

"As promised." He winked at Lily, who was

starving. She stuffed an entire pancake into her mouth—it was like biting into the most delicious, spongiest cloud.

Guru Jasmine turned toward the young Gems. "I am proud of each of you. By joining forces, you've grown into a wonderful team."

"Magic Gems *shore* are stronger when we stick together!" Lily's dad joked, making everyone giggle.

"He's right." Guru Jasmine chuckled. "Pebbles will be strong again because of your bravery, determination, and teamwork." She then turned to Lily. "Shall we see what form your gemstone chooses?" Her sea-blue eyes twinkled.

Guru Jasmine opened her palm, and Lily placed her sapphire gemstone inside it. Closing her fingers over the sapphire, her mother cast a spell. Lily's gemstone transformed into a pair of beautiful blue earrings.

Lily looked away, feeling embarrassed.

"What's wrong, Lilydew?" her mother asked.

"You said I was brave, but for most of the journey, I wasn't. I was nervous and scared. So why did I earn my gemstone?"

Guru Jasmine cupped Lily's face. "Being brave means doing something even when you're afraid. You can be brave *and* scared at the same time."

"In fact, I'd be worried if you *weren't* scared sailing through the marshlands and the Inky Lagoon," her dad said with a shiver.

"We've always been proud of you, Lilydew," said Guru Jasmine. "You never give up, even when things get tough. You had to think fast on your tail to find clever ways to solve the problems and dangers you faced. Through it all, you stayed loyal to Pebbles, your friends, and even yourself. That is true courage and the mark of a Magic Gem."

Lily couldn't help but smile. She might still be

scared of the dark, the deep, and the unknown. But now she knew she was also brave.

"Everyone, Pebbles is awake!" yelled Rio.

Lily rushed over to find the baby otter sitting in his basket with a confused look that said, *Why am I in a basket and not in the water?*

Pari covered him in lick-kisses. Everyone laughed as he wriggled free and splashed into the water, kicking with his healed paw.

Lily, Rio, Imara, and Scarlett jumped in after him. Cotton and the other pups joined too. Using her magic, Lily created small waves for the otters to chase and slide down. Pebbles squealed the loudest!

Soon, the sun rose, painting the sky in golden brushstrokes. The air rang with laughter.

Lily twirled on her tailfins. The Magic Gems had saved the day!

Read more Magic Gems!

MAGIC GEMS

Can Rio rescue a missing chipmunk and earn his first gemstone? Turn the page for a special sneak peek!

Rio slowed. It was time to call on his magic.

In a quiet clearing where the trees stood farther apart, Rio crouched on all fours and took a deep breath. The smell of moss, roots, and leaves filled his lungs.

Whoosh!

Ribbons of green sparkles swirled out of him. His arms and legs stretched, slender and strong, tipped with shiny golden hooves. A dazzling green horn bloomed from his forehead, dusted with glittering pollen. Flowers blossomed in his mane and tail, filling the air with the scent of a spring meadow.

Magic shimmered through Rio.

He was no longer a boy.

He had transformed into a majestic unicorn.

Instantly, the forest exploded into color. Leaves shone like liquid emeralds. Flowers shimmered like rainbows in the sun. Birds sang in a chorus of chirpy twitters. With his unicorn senses, Rio could see sharper, smell more clearly, and hear for miles.

Time to find you, whisperbloom.

Lowering his nose, he sniffed the ground.

THUMP!

Something landed on his back. He turned, rearing up on his hind legs, and came face-to-face with a fluffy cloudtail bunny.

About the Author

Payal Doshi loves writing about magic, adventure, and extraordinary creatures. If she could transform like the Magic Gems in her stories, she'd be a friendly dragon with giant pink wings! Born in Mumbai, India, Payal now lives in Minneapolis, Minnesota, with her husband and daughter. When she's not writing, she can be found nose-deep in a book, sipping coffee, or dreaming up fantastical worlds where a sprinkle of magic is always in the air. Learn more about Payal and her books at payaldoshiauthor.com.